LET LIBERTY RISE!

HOW AMERICA'S SCHOOLCHILDREN

HELPED SAVE THE STATUE OF LIBERTY

BY **Chana Stiefel**

ILLUSTRATED BY **Chuck Groenink**

SCHOLASTIC PRESS ★ NEW YORK

It was America's 100th Birthday!

The people of France were building a giant gift for their friends in the United States.

It was an enormous
statue — one of the
largest the world was yet to see!

Her name was **Liberty**.

With her torch held high,
she was a symbol of freedom and
friendship between the two countries.

But she was too big to send in one piece.
So all 350 pieces of **Lady Liberty**, from
the tips of her toes to the rays of her crown,
were placed in crates — 214 in all — and
packed together in the hull of a ship.

"*Bon voyage*!" the French people cried, when the ship *Isère* set sail across the Atlantic. It was the spring of 1885.

One month later, the **Statue of Liberty** arrived at New York's Bedloe's Island.

Soon, workers were hoisting the heavy crates from the ship. They marveled at this gargantuan gift.

But a colossal problem had been brewing. The French had asked the Americans to build a pedestal — a huge footstool for the statue to stand on. And it was barely half built when she arrived.

When a statue weighs nearly as much as 40 elephants, she needs a strong foundation to hold her up.

But funds for the pedestal had dried up. And few Americans wanted to pay the bill.

Her pedestal would cost more than $100,000 to complete. (That's $2.6 million today — enough to buy 203,000 kids' tickets to **Lady Liberty**'s crown.) Even New York's richest millionaires turned up their noses.

What kind of gift is that?

Without a pedestal, **Lady Liberty** would never rise.

Like a giant 350-piece puzzle, crates still packed with her parts would be scattered about Bedloe's Island in the scorching sun and pounding rain.

Poor **Lady Liberty**!

And even though **Lady Liberty** had a mouth — a huge mouth, stretching three feet wide — she needed a voice to get that pedestal built!

Send her home to Paris!

Ugh!

That voice came from a man named Joseph Pulitzer. Like **Lady Liberty**, Pulitzer sailed to America from a foreign shore, arriving as a poor Jewish Hungarian immigrant when he was 17. He taught himself English, fought for the Union in the Civil War, and worked as a lumberjack, waiter, lawyer, politician, and newspaperman.

Eventually, Pulitzer bought a newspaper called the *New York World*. Two months before **Lady Liberty** set sail, he knew she had to stand in New York Harbor, the gateway to America. When he heard about her plight, he was furious. Pulitzer wrote in the *World*:

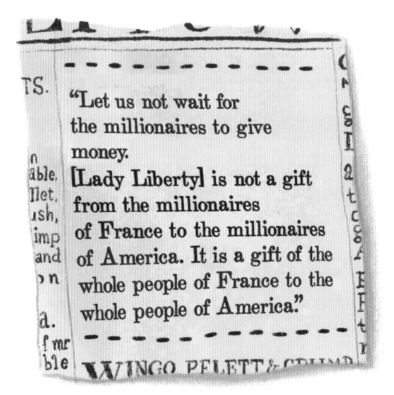

"Let us not wait for the millionaires to give money. [Lady Liberty] is not a gift from the millionaires of France to the millionaires of America. It is a gift of the whole people of France to the whole people of America."

Then Pulitzer made a tantalizing offer: The *World* would print the name of every person who donated to the pedestal fund, no matter how small the sum — or how small the person.

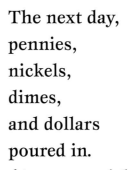

Extra! Extra! Read all about it!

The next day, pennies, nickels, dimes, and dollars poured in. (A penny might not seem like much, but every cent in those days would be worth about 26 cents today. One dollar would equal about $26.)

Newspapers across the country picked up the story.

Schoolchildren everywhere emptied their piggy banks. In the first week, the *World* raised more than $2,000!

As weeks passed, more and more money rolled in.

A young girl sent in 60 cents. "I wish I could make it $60,000," she wrote, "but drops make an ocean."

A "poor office boy" contributed a hard-earned nickel.

Dear Sir,
I'm it a poor

Children from one family wrote that they had taken French lessons.

"We love the good French people for giving us this beautiful statue and we send you $1, the money we saved to go to the circus."

Addie M. Berryman wrote,
"We are 14 little boys and
girls and we made up a
club for the Pedestal
Fund . . . Instead of
spending our money for
candy, we saved up. I made
up this letter myself.
I am the president."

Two boys wrote, "When we get to be big men, we want to say we helped build the pedestal . . . We now send you $13. Maybe we will have more."

Twelve public schools in Trenton, New Jersey, collected $105.07.

A kindergarten class from Davenport, Iowa, mailed in $1.35.

In June, a $10 donation came from 1,000 students. Each child gave a penny a week for charity. That week, they sent their pennies to help build the pedestal.

Every day, the money poured in. Every day, they were closer to reaching their goal.

mr Joseph Pulitzer
the World Newspaper
New York NY

Finally, on August 11, 1885, the *World*'s headline read:

"ONE HUNDRED THOUSAND DOLLARS!"

Thanks to 120,000 donors — schoolchildren, as well as farmers, factory workers, policemen, immigrants, housewives, office clerks, and others — **Lady Liberty** reached her goal. "The honorable rich as well as the poorest of the poor . . . jointed in common spirit for a common cause," Pulitzer proudly wrote in the *World*.

CLAMS
5¢

At last, there would be enough money to finish the pedestal! It wasn't just a footstool for **Lady Liberty** to stand on. With concrete walls 20 feet thick and 89 feet tall, it would become a magnificent anchor for the statue to weather the test of time.

Once the pedestal was finished, **Lady Liberty**
was freed from her crates. Slowly, piece by piece,
she started to rise. First, workers assembled her
metal skeleton. Then they riveted her copper "skin."

Up,

up,

up

rose the statue,
until she was
complete.

On October 28, 1886, about one million people came to celebrate **Lady Liberty**'s inauguration. A parade passed by Pulitzer's *World* building. And soon, everyone would see what America's pennies had built.

There she stood, tall and proud, the **Statue of Liberty**, America's symbol of freedom and hope.

After the celebrations, steamships carrying new immigrants sailed into New York Harbor. Holding her torch high, the **Statue of Liberty** welcomed them to their new home.

And there she stands today, thanks to the contributions of people all across America — and children just like you.

Timeline

1865 ★ French scholar Édouard de Laboulaye proposes the idea of a monument representing liberty to the sculptor Frédéric-Auguste Bartholdi.

1871 ★ Bartholdi tours America from coast to coast. He chooses Bedloe's Island in New York Harbor—the gateway to America—as the perfect spot for his giant masterpiece.

1876 ★ The French begin construction of the statue. At a celebration for America's 100th birthday in Philadelphia, Bartholdi offers a sneak peek. He displays Liberty's finished right arm and torch. People pay 50 cents to climb up to the copper balcony under the flame and take in the view.

1877 ★ An American committee sets up a Pedestal Fund to raise money for building the pedestal.

1879 ★ Alexandre-Gustave Eiffel, a famous French engineer, designs an internal framework to make the Statue of Liberty stand.

1880 ★ The French people collect $250,000 to build the Statue of Liberty.

1881 ★ American architect Richard Morris Hunt is hired to design the pedestal.

1883 ★ The poet Emma Lazarus writes the now world-famous sonnet called "The New Colossus" for an auction to raise money for the Pedestal Fund. Deeply moved by the harrowing plight of immigrants escaping persecution, she was inspired to write the poem.
★ General Charles P. Stone, a military engineer, is hired to build the pedestal and its foundation.

1884 ★ Workers in Paris complete the construction of the Statue of Liberty.

1885 ★ (January) Workers in Paris start to dismantle the Statue of Liberty to ship her to America. During that time, funds for the construction of the pedestal run out.
★ (March 16) Joseph Pulitzer launches the *World*'s Pedestal Campaign, offering to print the name of every donor in his newspaper.
★ (May 21) Liberty sets sail for America aboard the *Isère*.

★ (June 17) Liberty arrives at New York Harbor. Only half of the pedestal is constructed.

★ (August 11) The *World*'s Pedestal Campaign reaches its goal of $100,000. Construction of the pedestal moves toward completion.

1886 ★ (April 22) The last stone is laid in the pedestal. Construction of the statue begins.

★ (July 12) The first copper plates are riveted to the statue's internal iron frame.

★ (August 3) Congress approves funding of $56,500 for the Statue of Liberty's completion and inauguration.

★ (October 28) One million people attend the inauguration of the Statue of Liberty in New York City.

★ (November 1) The torch is lit. Fireworks light up the sky over New York City.

1903 ★ Emma Lazarus's poem, "The New Colossus," is added to the statue's pedestal.

1924 ★ The Statue of Liberty is declared a national monument.

1956 ★ Bedloe's Island is renamed Liberty Island.

1986 ★ Restoration of the statue is completed for her 100th birthday.

2001 ★ The Statue of Liberty closes temporarily after the September 11th attacks.

2004 ★ The pedestal is reopened to the public with new security measures.

2020 ★ Like many other national monuments, the Statue of Liberty closes temporarily due to the COVID-19 pandemic.

About four million people have visited the Statue of Liberty every year.

More about the Statue of Liberty

★ Bedloe's Island (now known as Liberty Island) is the site of the Statue of Liberty. Prior to the arrival of Europeans in the 16th century, the original inhabitants of the area were various Native American tribes, who lived there as early as 783 AD. It is likely that several tribes, including the Manahatin, Munsee, and Lenape, visited the island for different reasons, including to harvest oysters. The Lenape named it Minnissais, or Lesser Island.

★ French scholar Édouard de Laboulaye, who first proposed the idea of the Statue of Liberty, felt that the American Civil War and the abolishment of slavery were hard-won victories for freedom and democracy. He suggested that the Statue of Liberty would be a symbol of American ideals and a beacon of hope for the French, who still dreamed of a democratic government of their own.

★ The statue was originally called "Liberty Enlightening the World."

★ Bartholdi originally intended that the Statue of Liberty would work as a lighthouse, but the light in her torch was never bright enough.

★ Broken chains lie at Liberty's feet, a symbol of the broken shackles of tyranny. She appears to be walking, with her right foot in mid-stride.

★ The date of America's Declaration of Independence is inscribed in Roman numerals on the tablet held in Liberty's left arm: July IV, MDCCLXXVI (July 4, 1776).

★ Two hundred thousand pounds of copper were used to build the Statue of Liberty. Copper can be bent and shaped without cracking. It cannot rust.

★ The Statue of Liberty was originally the color of a copper penny. But copper naturally forms a green film (called "patina"). Some of the exposed outer layer is protected from dampness and corrosion, but damage did occur. It took about 30 years for the statue to turn green.

★ The thickness of Liberty's copper skin is 3/32 of an inch, the thickness of two pennies.

★ Laying the foundation of the pedestal took eight and a half months and used 24,000 barrels of cement. It was the largest concrete block in existence at the time, measuring 91 square feet on the bottom and 65 square feet at the top.

⭐ The cost of the pedestal, originally thought to be $100,000, jumped to over $320,000 once construction began. Individual citizens and Congress helped foot the remainder of the bill. Money was still needed for an electrical system and planning an inauguration. Congress approved the final $56,500 on August 3, 1886.

⭐ When the Statue of Liberty was completed in 1886, she was one of the tallest structures in the Western World. At 305 feet and 1 inch, she was the tallest structure in New York. (This measurement is from the ground to the tip of her torch.)

⭐ Inside the Statue of Liberty are 354 steps leading up to the crown.

Bibliography

Brian, Denis. *Pulitzer: A Life*. New York: John Wiley & Sons, 2001.

Harris, Jonathan. *The First 100 Years of the Statue of Liberty*. New York: Four Winds Press, 1985.

Mitchell, Elizabeth. *Liberty's Torch: The Great Adventure to Build the Statue of Liberty*. New York: Atlantic Monthly Press, 2014.

Moreno, Barry. *The Statue of Liberty Encyclopedia*. New York: Simon & Schuster, 2000.

Sutherland, Cara. *The Statue of Liberty*. Museum of the City of New York, Barnes and Noble, 2003.

Books for Young Readers:

Byrd, Robert. *Liberty Arrives! How America's Grandest Statue Found Her Home*. New York: Dial Books for Young Readers: An imprint of Penguin Random House LLC, 2019.

Friddell, Claudia. *Saving Lady Liberty: Joseph Pulitzer's Fight for the Statue of Liberty*. Illustrated by Stacy Innerst. Calkins Creek, 2020.

Glasthal, Jacqueline B. & Reingold, Alan. *Liberty on 23rd Street*. New York: Silver Moon Press, 2006.

Stevens, Carla & Ray, Deborah Kogan. *Lily and Miss Liberty*. New York: Scholastic Inc., 1992.

Web sites:

http://www.nps.gov/stli/learn/historyculture/pulitzer-in-depth.htm

https://www.nps.gov/stli/learn/historyculture/places_creating_statue.htm

https://www.nps.gov/stli/planyourvisit/basicinfo.htm

https://www.nps.gov/stli/planyourvisit/get-the-facts.htm

https://www.statueofliberty.org/statue-of-liberty/overview-history/

https://www.history.com/topics/landmarks/statue-of-liberty

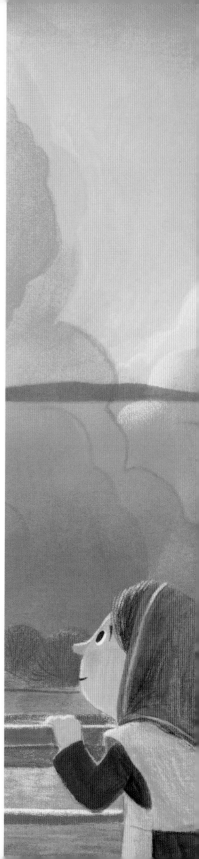

FRÉDÉRIC-AUGUSTE BARTHOLDI (1834–1904), THE FRENCH SCULPTOR WHO CREATED THE STATUE OF LIBERTY AS A GIFT TO THE UNITED STATES.

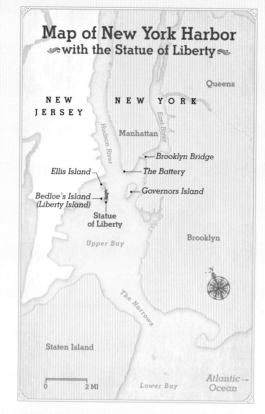

Map of New York Harbor
⁓ with the Statue of Liberty ⁓

Queens

NEW JERSEY   NEW YORK

Manhattan

Hudson River

East River

→ Brooklyn Bridge
→ The Battery
→ Governors Island

Ellis Island

Bedloe's Island (Liberty Island)
Statue of Liberty

Upper Bay

Brooklyn

The Narrows

Staten Island

0   2 MI

Lower Bay   Atlantic Ocean →

IN 1871, BARTHOLDI CHOSE BEDLOE'S ISLAND (NOW KNOWN AS LIBERTY ISLAND), THE GATEWAY TO AMERICA, FOR THE SITE OF THE STATUE OF LIBERTY.

A LOOK BACK IN TIME

LIBERTY'S TORCH AND PART OF HER ARM WERE DISPLAYED AT THE 1876 CENTENNIAL EXHIBITION IN PHILADELPHIA TO STIR UP EXCITEMENT FOR FUNDRAISING. PEOPLE PAID TO CLIMB THROUGH THE ARM AND STAND ON THE TORCH'S PLATFORM. (LEFT-AND RIGHT-EYE IMAGES IN PHOTO CREATE THE ILLUSION OF A 3-D IMAGE WHEN VIEWED THROUGH A STEREOSCOPE.)

CRAFTSMEN FIRST BUILT MODELS OF THE STATUE OF LIBERTY IN BARTHOLDI'S WAREHOUSE IN PARIS, FRANCE (APPROX: WINTER, 1882).

WORKMEN CONSTRUCTED A WOODEN SKELETON OF THE LEFT ARM AND HAND OF THE STATUE OF LIBERTY, AND THEN COVERED IT IN PLASTER (PARIS, 1883). MODELS LIKE THIS WERE USED TO GRADUALLY BUILD THE STATUE TO SCALE. THE FULL-SCALE SKELETON OF THE STATUE OF LIBERTY IS MADE OF IRON, COVERED WITH COPPER SKIN.

In 1885, Joseph Pulitzer (1847–1911), owner of the *New York World* newspaper, spearheaded a fundraising campaign to build the pedestal for the Statue of Liberty. By printing the name of each individual (including children) who contributed at least a penny to the pedestal, he raised over $100,000 toward the pedestal fund.

Pieces of the statue were popular tourist attractions while the work was under construction.

The Statue of Liberty was constructed in Paris from 1881 to 1884. At 15 stories high, the statue — surrounded by scaffolding — towered over the rooftops of Paris. It became a popular tourist attraction, before being shipped to America in 350 pieces in 1885.

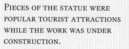

The nearly-completed pedestal of the Statue of Liberty, designed by Richard Morris Hunt, is shown under construction in 1886.

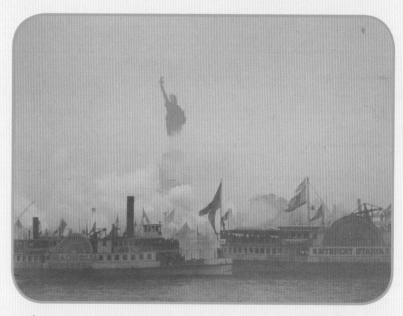

About one million people attended the inauguration of the Statue of Liberty on October 28, 1886. The overcast, drizzly day began with a grand parade in Manhattan, followed by a flotilla celebration in New York Harbor (shown here), and a dedication ceremony presided by President Grover Cleveland, with an unveiling of the statue on Bedloe's Island.

In memory of Jackie Glasthal, who stood
for liberty, equality, and friendship. –C.S.

For all immigrant kids big and small –C.G.

PHOTOS ©:
38 top left: Archives Of American Art, Smithsonian Institution
38 top center: Jim McMahon/Mapman ®
38 top right: Library of Congress
38 bottom left: Library of Congress
38 bottom right: New York Public Library
39 top left: Mary Evans Picture Library/age fotostock
39 top center: National Park Service, Statue of Liberty National Monument and Ellis Island
39 top right: National Park Service, Statue of Liberty National Monument and Ellis Island
39 bottom left background: National Archives
39 bottom center: Library of Congress
39 bottom right: Library of Congress
40 bottom left: University of California, Berkeley
40 top right: Detroit Publishing Co./Library of Congress

ACKNOWLEDGMENTS:
THANK YOU TO BARRY MORENO AND JEFF DOSIK AT THE BOB HOPE
MEMORIAL LIBRARY ON ELLIS ISLAND FOR THEIR ASSISTANCE WITH
MY RESEARCH, MY EDITOR DIANNE HESS AT SCHOLASTIC FOR HER
DEDICATION AND ATTENTION TO DETAIL, MY LATE FRIEND JACKIE GLASTHAL
(THE INSPIRATION FOR THIS STORY), AND MY WONDERFUL FAMILY FOR LIVING
WITH ALL THINGS LIBERTY FOR THE PAST FEW YEARS.—C.S.

SPECIAL THANKS TO DAVID LOVETT FOR HIS METICULOUS FACT CHECKING,
TO DENNIS ZOTIGH, CULTURAL SPECIALIST, SMITHSONIAN NATIONAL
MUSEUM OF THE AMERICAN INDIAN, AND JOSH VOGEL, GALLERY MANAGER
AT THE SKYSCRAPER MUSEUM.

AUTHOR'S NOTE: FIGURES FOR THE COMPARATIVE COST OF THE PEDESTAL
AND TICKETS TO LIBERTY'S CROWN ARE BASED ON CALCULATIONS FROM
2019, AND ARE SUBJECT TO FLUCTUATION.

> **To the Editor of The World:**
> I am a boy nine years old and I have earned 25
> cents and my sister Ina earned 15 cents and ma
> gave my baby sister Amy 10 cents; 25 and 15 and
> 10 equal 50 cents for the pedestal fund.
> RALPH, INA and AMY MADDEN.

FROM THE *WORLD*, JUNE 20, 1885.

THE STATUE OF LIBERTY IN NEW YORK HARBOR, ABOUT 1905.

★ Text copyright © 2021 by Chana Stiefel ★ Illustrations © 2021 by Chuck Groenink ★
All rights reserved. Published by Scholastic Press, an imprint of Scholastic Inc., *Publishers since 1920.* SCHOLASTIC, SCHOLASTIC PRESS, and associated logos are trademarks and/or registered trademarks of Scholastic Inc. ★ The publisher does not have any control over and does not assume any responsibility for author or third-party websites or their content. ★ No part of this publication may be reproduced, stored in a retrieval system, or transmitted in any form or by any means, electronic, mechanical, photocopying, recording, or otherwise, without written permission of the publisher. For information regarding permission, write to Scholastic Inc., Attention: Permissions Department, 557 Broadway, New York, NY 10012 ★ Library of Congress Cataloging-in-Publication Data ★ Names: Stiefel, Chana, 1968- author. | Groenink, Chuck, illustrator. ★ Title: Let Liberty Rise : how America's schoolchildren helped save the Statue of Liberty / by Chana Stiefel ; illustrated by Chuck Groenink. ★ Description: First edition. | New York : Scholastic Press, 2021. | Includes bibliographical references. | Audience: Ages 6–8. | Audience: Grades 2–3. | Summary: "The true story of how schoolchildren helped fund the construction of the pedestal for the Statue of Liberty in New York City."— Provided by publisher. Identifiers: LCCN 2020003528 | ISBN 9781338225884 (hardback) Subjects: LCSH: Statue of Liberty (New York, N.Y.)—History—Juvenile literature. | New York (N.Y.)—Buildings, structures, etc.—Juvenile literature. Classification: LCC F128.64.L6 S748 2021 | DDC 974.7/1—dc23 ★
10 9 8 7 6 5 4 3 2 1   21 22 23 24 25 ★ Printed in China   38 ★ First edition, March 2021 ★ Chuck Groenink's illustrations were created with gouache, pencils, and Photoshop. ★ The text type was set in ITC Esprit Std Book. ★ The display type was set in Miltonian Tatoo Regular. ★ The book was printed on 128 gsm matte art paper and bound at RR Donnelley Asia. ★ Production was overseen by Jael Fogle. ★ Manufacturing was supervised by Shannon Rice. ★ The book was art directed and designed by Marijka Kostiw and edited by Dianne Hess. ★